PLANET OF ME
UNIVERSE OF US

Tiffany Nicole Pigée is a gifted poet and creative storyteller. Crafting ballads and symphonies with her words, she gives voice to the intimate experiences of human connection and of loss and of redemption. She focuses on creating literary landscapes to explore and confront thoughts and emotions often left unsaid.

Tiffany Nicole is the author of On My Best Day, Planet of Me Universe of Us and is currently finalizing her third poetry and prose collection for release in 2023. She lives with her husband and a growing collection of fiddle leaf figs.

Planet of Me Universe of Us

TIFFANY NICOLE PIGÉE

ISBN 9781737510826

Printed in the United States of America

22 23 24 25 26   7 6 5 4 3 2 1

Cover Design and Interior Layout by: Melvin Pigée

for the lovers...

who love earnestly and fiercely -
without regard or restriction,
satiated only by the most intense emotion -
those of us who feel everything

may we find our way to the safe space
of vulnerability and care
may we find our way to the comfort
that only true love provides

protostar

let me take your breath away

don't love me because
i'm what you've been searching for,
the exact manifestation of your dreams.

because i fit the mold, smile just right
and tilt my head perfectly when i laugh -

>   *just as you envisioned*

i am not a standard edition.
i am the exception. *the exemption*

the one that decimates your thoughts
leaving you uncomfortable, unsure
of your own capacity

i want to be the one that ravages your heart
the one who causes you to question
the whole idea of love

let me be your choke hold.
the one that takes your breath away.
leaving you in a struggle

gasping. heaving... *breathless*

young love

i remember
when we were
intensely connected
body and soul. entangled
completely together
immersed in each other
lost... in the haze
of love

old diaries mummify a version of us we'd rather forget

i never had a soft cover journal
until i was full grown. hard covers last longer,
weather better.

old diaries left in boxes. packed away,
become graveyards. entombed recollections
of young love and secret crushes

mummified scribbles. prayers
and petitions for death to set me free
from gut-wrenching heartache.

overflowing and faded pages
of the most dramatic of eulogies

please don't cry
for the abandoned heart
of a 17-year-old girl.
decimated by true love given
but not returned.

question

if i lost myself
while finding you
did i really lose
anything at all?

please don't jinx this

don't start... with me
already thinking of the end,
imagining a day
when there's no us.

just be here, now.

immersed in this moment.
where i am loving you
and you are loving me

the devastation of first loves

the first time i felt someone,
deeply. not in the flesh. no,
not in the body. not on my skin.
maybe on my skin. yes,
and maybe in my body too.

the first time i was set a flame. i was ignited. lit

my first experience, a soul connection.
the most unexplainable encounter,
felt like a spiritual awakening.
my heart failed its hold on itself.
and i lost control *of myself.*

thought i had a handle on it.
        knew i had a handle on it.

didn't have a handle on it.
        never had a handle on it.

nothing needed | everything missing

she is everything
you are missing and
nothing you need

a feeling
pure energy
an irresistible sensation

she sings without words. a siren
to your soul. beguiling
your heart. to captivity. enslaving
your body. to her bidding

and you are powerless
to the exquisite seduction.
of her. wholly vulnerable
to her lure

an attraction
an inebriation
a relentless temptation

you are nothing
she needs and
everything she is missing

nothing makes sense

there's difficulty with my tongue lately.
i'm having trouble communicating
my thoughts.

it's heavy, in a way i can't explain properly,
especially when they are about you.
and lately, they are always about you

let me light the way

in this universe, of us,
let me be a sun.
or a moon.
maybe, a star

let me be the source
of illumination
for your infiniteness

the light
to every dark place
revealing the beauty
hidden and unknown

exposing the countless veiled gems
and gifts. and blessings.
blind to your eyes
before loving *me*

you didn't leave me in wonder
of what could have been

you didn't lock eyes
and smile
and walk away

didn't pass me by
and leave me in wonder
of what could have been

you glanced
you spoke
you stayed awhile

and i haven't been the same
since that day…
since the very moment
we first met

true connection exists despite the body

being with her
is more about you
being present

in heart and soul and spirit

than ever has it been
about your actual and
physical presence

supernova

lust is always two steps ahead

let's just stay here in the thick of it
in the seductive tangle
of one another.

before our minds catch up with our bodies
and we realize we have fallen.
but not for love. but not in love.

for something else, entirely.

you and i

i awaken in bliss

limbs entangled
synchronized breath

a foreign vibration in my heart

shy memories
of the night before
of you. and i

and i think i am
in love
with you. and i

i am
young and pliable
wild and free
all and nothing,
in your presence.

shared whispers of ecstasy
words laced with poetry

as you seiche
my soul. with the seeds
of you. and i

the memory of us is not enough

i often wish i could still feel you.
the touch of your skin. the kiss
of your lips. the way you grip
my thighs. my neck.
and the small of my back

it's not enough
to have experienced all of you
when i am here, ravenously hungry
to taste you again. to swallow you
into the whole of me.

i need you.
i need to - immerse myself
in your intimate places. gorge
on the limbs, the tongue, the flesh
of you

i realize now,
the memory of us
is not enough
to satiate my desire

i don't want to remember
how you made me feel.
i want to *feel*
how i remember you.

create poetry in me

take me to the most beautiful destinations

> *i want to see life through your eyes*

tell me how i make you feel

> *create poetry in my body and my mind*

make love to me in unfamiliar places

> *i want to feel you in the sky*

design a home in my heart

> *a sanctuary, strong enough for the test of time*

illusion of love

lost in your whimsy.
intoxicated by the aroma of you.
entrenched in this fabric
that covers your body.

let me sojourn here,
insulated from what is real.
in this place,
wedged between lust and fantasy
where reality is of no consequence.
and the weight of the world escapes my grasp
and my only need,

       my only want,

              my only desire,

     is you.

a heavenly experience

let's make love like the gods
uninhibited. exotic. and free
we'll climax in the clouds
for all the stars to see

the things that happen when we happen

our bodies liaise
when we make love
a secret language
a seductive tongue

communing
in perfect harmony
as we coalesce
from two into one

only you know the language of us

words elude thought
when you speak to my body
when you talk *that* talk.
in our secret dialect

the private seductive language of us

can't quite grasp how your tongue
knows just what to say
how your mouth whispers commands
and my flesh eagerly obeys

when you say my name
the way only you enunciate me.
setting off an electric response,
upending everything

a complete eruption of ecstasy

not at all sure how you do
what you do. to me
but please, baby, please
don't stop

somewhere our love is remembered

there's a sandy beach
on the coast. near Savannah.
a quiet little place
where our bodies first met
and our mouths fell vulnerable
to *i love you.*

you say you don't recall.
your mind fails this memory
but i know that you know.

and i'm sure,
the shoreline still remembers
our kisses. fully confident,
if you look hard enough,
there's a permanent imprint,
of us, somewhere forgotten
beneath the sand.

it is there,
when the tides come in,
we are still lovers.

it is there,
when the sun sets
we are still in love.

the invasion of me

before you left,
you settled into my body
lips first. sunk your taste
deep into my mouth

and now that you're gone,
i can't get enough
of the zest that lingers inside

so, i don't eat much
anymore. too afraid,
my tongue will forget
the distinct flavor of you

the melodies you left behind

when i'm with you
it seems, my tongue
is only versed in poetry

in your absence
it sings the lyrics
of the ballads
you left inside me

creating music
with the words
you kissed into my mouth
melodies, for the songs
you left behind

solar flare

the real reason i keep coming back

every time i feel
a little better, i return
to let you break me again.

because i've realized
that if it all comes together,
i'll have to face myself.

and honestly,
despising you
is so much easier for me.

some love lessons we can do without

in the 2nd grade
~~i thought~~ i had a boyfriend,
named Milton.

i used to write *i love Milton,*
inside cut out hearts, i drew with crayon
on colored construction paper

i wasn't allowed to talk to boys. so i snuck
to call him. once. when my mother was away

can i be your girlfriend Milton?

    you can be my third girlfriend

i don't want to be number three

    i already have one, no, two… and Crystal
    will be after you

a narcissist doesn't want you to stay, they just don't want you to go

i sat. shaking.
listening. grieving, the words
of closure you spoke so nonchalantly.
blaming me for *your* transgressions
taunting me with what we could have been
if only, i had acted accordingly.

i despise your voice
present and past. in this moment.

you've declared these words
so many times, before.
and will again, of this i'm sure.

still, i can't stop listening
to each tortured syllable.
every -

i wish i'd never met you

i sat. trembling.
as your words, turned grey,
becoming inaudible groans.
my mind lost,
in the comprehension. hiding,
in the safety of failed understanding

i need to go – i whisper

and quiet stills *everything*
confusion floods your face.
disappointed, i've ruined your expectation -

surprised, you wonder out loud *if i heard you*

i stood to leave. you stood too.
urgently pleading with your eyes now.
as you drop to your knees
and bury your head in my thighs.

> *don't go.*
> *i need you* – you utter

and we both know,

> *it will always be this way.*

monogamy

"it isn't natural
we're not meant to love just one, for forever.
monogamy is suffocating.
binding ourselves to a single soul
strips away our freedom.
leaves us powerless and caged.
i don't understand how you could see things differently" –

he spoke in a low tone. almost soothing
a lullaby of careful execution
charm meant to permeate my beliefs

he looked genuinely confused
that i was still. that i was quiet. blank faced
and attentive

i pondered his sentiments. closed my eyes
and thought long and hard on his words
envisioned myself a goddess. a queen
with many suitors. entangled
in the most sensual affairs

i ruled with my prowess. a master seductress
riding transient lust to celestial peaks

it was a sight! the most vivid dream.

oh, how easily the mind is swayed by reason

he *almost* convinced me
my heart could dwell unscathed
among countless lovers
in infinite universes and still remain whole

i wondered if these were the thoughts
of his father and all the men
that have disappointed loyal women

the ones that always return
to confess their mistake. to plead
for forgiveness. to sob
for reconciliation

the ones who realize much too late
that there is complete freedom
and ecstasy in the fullness of love,

even if lonely, empty, useless men
taught them differently

what is love without war?

i'm not sure how love works
this way. without pain. without sacrifice.
without complete and utter confusion

who loves like this?

please, bear with me.
as i navigate this new way
of loving someone - new

peace, is unfamiliar to my heart

i learned love differently, you see.
never whole. always pieces
of me and them, broken.
hard to match. even harder to piece together

and what is love without war anyway?

a battle to the death,
is what i know well

i'm a fast learner though.
but you'll have to go slow
so that i can fight the urge
to attack

the potential of someone is not enough

potential is a deceitful thing
a dangerous lure to be tempted by
oh, the chaos lost hopes will bring
when nothing manifests at sunrise

the chaos of trauma bonding

love that is not love but feels like love
or maybe lust, is like combat.

> *it is wild and untamed and destructive.*
> *lost. found. possessed and unclaimed.*
> *passion and intensity and sorrow and pain.*
> *a hemorrhage of emotion*

it is not about you. it is all about you,
trivial and petty and dense and provocative.

it cannot be contained. it aches to be contained.
it must be contained. in you.
by you

it is poison and elixir.
enough. and not enough.
at times, too damn much.

> *always, too damn much*

it smells like many, feels like one.
tragic and deceiving, all at once.

the truths that exist inside the lies

he doesn't know -

or doesn't want to know

your charm wasn't birthed
from innocence

you are a universe of experiences.
a proper student.
knowing just what to say
where to touch
how it makes him feel

he finds you intoxicating,
loosing himself in your spell of drunkenness

loves the inebriation

unaware it's all fantasy
this can never be real

he makes excuses.

finds reasons to explain
why he can't stay away,
to justify his absence from her.

because when he is with you
he is absent from her

reminds himself in whispers
why he should leave.
says he can't help himself. tells you -

> *it should have been you*
> *you are star-crossed. cursed.*
> *he wishes he'd found you first*
> *stumbled upon you in his youth*
> *made different decisions*

and you stare, at the ceiling,
at the hairline crack in the upper right corner.
because, this happens every. single. time

guilt raises up through his throat
and his words fail his thoughts.
he has made you his prison,
convinced himself you are an escape.

and he unknowingly is yours

because somewhere between the greeting
and the payment
you lose yourself too.
forgetting who you once were
who you should have been
who you desired to be

he provides a temporary reprieve
from the weight of the demons
riding your neck like shadows.
spirits, with incessant reminders

the whispers, only you can hear

"this isn't the life you were meant for my dear"

and you stare at the ceiling
his voice fading,
like distant music in the background,
to the familiar words spoken
in your head.

you glare at the crack,
and silently answer back

oh, but it is
oh, but it is

non-committal negotiations

there is not enough of you

                there is too much of me

give me more us

                just not too much of we

it's time to retire the savior complex

i fell in love with you, saving me -
how you protected my heart and my mind,
brought me back from the edge

but i'm finding now
it is you who needs saving, *you see*
you seem to not understand

i was the one
you were meant to save
the first. the only. the last.
the end

war zone

in our home
combat was a past-time

we embarked
on the most brutal endeavors

nothing was sacred
nothing was spared

lover synonymous with adversary
friend indistinguishable from foe

we weaponized each other
in battle

war became the constant
tortuous cycle

a toxic sway
of love. war. forgive. attack

always,
love
war
forgive
attack

she lost her softness fighting
for what doesn't exist

she's been trying for so long
her softness is fast fading. worn.
tattered from this endless work

and though she is exhausted
rest evades her
because,

instead of surrendering
she fights
for a love
he will never return
an appreciation
he will never possess
a safe place for her
he will never be

if you are not enough, let her go

a woman only seeks
what she lacks. searching solely
for what she cannot find
within her complete self.

don't fault her
for your inability,
for your unwillingness
to be everything she needs

it is you who is not enough

it's time to let... her... go

you were always the best thing

when did he convince you
of his undeserving importance?

why did you allow yourself
to believe that he was the prize?

the war i'll never win

you dismantle me
with your words.
a vicious mental war
waged on each other.

one, i seem to always lose.

yet here i am, battling.
knowing when it's all over,
i'll be the one nursing my own wounds,
again.

delighted and amused

i was drowning
in the chaos
of you and i. choking
on the disappointment
cascading down my throat

fought my way to the surface
seeking momentary peace. love.
you

only to be pulled under by insensitivity
and manipulation. and empty words.

and i could clearly see you there,
on the other side
of the shallow water,
watching. looming.
flush with excitement
at the view

a front row seat
to the demise of me

promises are just words

i memorialized the words you whispered
when laying alone with me.
pillow talk moments, i deemed sacred
and convinced myself to believe

you said this was forever
and nothing could take you away from me.
you said we'd spend a lifetime of lifetimes together
promises you knew you'd never keep

sometimes it's easier to be who you need

i found this life
easier to stomach
when i lost myself in you.

when i realized being
who you needed
was so much simpler

than who i needed me to be

the signs are always there

i was so in love
with the idea of us,
i fooled myself
a thousand times.
purposefully ignoring
the ugly chaotic mayhem
we actually were
together

solstice

a little less of this, a little more of that

this time, you tell me
i bore a hole through
your chest, right down past the bone.
to the marrow of you.

there's a distinct crack in your voice. a break
in the cadence. reminding me, of the distance
between us. making you too far away
to touch. too far away to comfort.
too far away to love.

and i'm a little disheveled now.
emotions knotted. as i listen
to your rainbow filtered words, pulling me in.
softly singing my soul's desire awake.
a siren. serenading,
my heart's demise. luring me
to slaughter.

> *we've been here before.*
> *it always ends the same*

and i wonder,
if this - is what is meant for us -

you on the other end of the line.
describing the terror of us
being apart. begging
for my return.
offering to send a ticket

and i wonder,
quietly to myself

why couldn't we be less tragic.
less star-crossed.
less Malört.

why weren't we more love story.
more soul mates.
more Chardonnay.

what goes unspoken can
bring the whole house down

what went unspoken still lingered, in the air.
seeping out invisible, on heavy sighs
and silent tears. and, the feelings coated
everything. formed a residue
of unreleased emotion.

and now, the unsaid is also the unseen.
slowly shattering the foundation
on which we were built.

hairline cracks
often go unnoticed. as they rage
beneath the surface. unchecked.
birthing black holes, continuously expanding,
like ripped tights at the knee.

and what we thought we could manage
            confident it was under control –
by pretending all was ideal, between us.
was already wreaking havoc. unraveling
the seams that once bound them together.
a volcano of emotion, ready to erupt

the confusion of us

i'm no longer sure
if what we had was love.
late night rendezvous
and ill-defined boundaries
straddle the line
on this one.

so many signs we ignored.
warning signals.

the shouting,
mistook for passion.
the other lovers,
we naively reconciled,
to each other, as friends.
the horrible words
we hurled at each other.

> *always landing in the sensitive places.*
> *always finding their way to the heart.*

maybe it was the elaborate stories
you'd tell. dramatic and convincing
in their deceit.

your why-don't-you-believe-me charm,

was the thorough manipulation, of me.

the alarms sounded in so many ways.
you muted sirens with emotional pleas.
talked me into an endless,
tortuous cycle.

i can't recognize the end
from the beginning. and now,
after all this time,
i'm still just as confused
as when i first started with you.

the heart forgets before the mind

i don't recognize you now
this disparate version of the same man.
though still familiar to my heart,
you are a stranger to my memory.

my mind holds a vision of you
long gone. i think. *i hope.*

one, you say, no longer exists.
but once did unbearable harm.

my heart trusts this new edition,
the enhanced version you now embody,
while my doubtful mind whispers
quietly, when you look away,

run

searching for the you i once knew

the you, i knew once
must still exist.
even though you try to convince me otherwise.

i find him in old text messages,
in photos i can't bear to delete,
in now crumpled love letters
    where he professed his forever love.

and although you keep telling me
you've always been this way,
that you haven't changed,
i know that not to be true.

and i'd bet the park bench,
where we shared our first kiss,
and the most intimate conversations
still remembers him too.

what could have been
doesn't exist in our story

i'm sure now, we annihilated one another
in our thoughts. all the terrible things
racing around in our heads. unchecked
and unfiltered. making *this*
~~dis~~connection unbearable.

and still, you find ways to remind me
of what could have been, of us.

> *but tell me, my love,*
> *which of us can predict*
> *the alternate ending of love lost?*

> *which of us can speak*
> *of a reality that never existed?*

i can't.

i'm still here,
beset by confusion.
trying to comprehend
what gave birth
to our downfall.

scavenging memories. endlessly
searching for the very moment
your heart left mine.

and you are somewhere
else. wandering
your own chaos.
apart from me.
lost, in the intricacies
of your own heart.

warring. for the unrealized potential, of us.

the very thing,
we somehow discarded.

the very thing,
we somehow forgot.

the imperfection of us makes
this harder than it should be

it's not easy being you
just as, i've discovered
it's not easy being me
and i've also come to realize
sometimes just *being*
anything at all
is difficult enough

and this is why this love is heavy.
not because we aren't perfect
for each other, *we are*

but because we struggle
with the imperfections in ourselves

making it difficult to fully comprehend
how someone else can love the damage
and the flaws, and all the wrong
that makes us, *us*

when they leave, the hardest
part comes after

this war, is an unfair battle
where you hold the high ground
of my heart. incessantly exploding my thoughts
with unsavory memories.
the ones i relentlessly try to forget

here, resides the turmoil
of my mind
and i am adrift

as i seek peace
despite your absence.
sifting through the rubble of my regret,
for actions and words i cannot alter

trying to make straight this labyrinth
to my heart. creating alternate realities
in my mind. where a perfected version of you
is here, with me

i hope one day, you find a love
like the love you could not give

a love that nurtures your expansion.
a love that heals your heart.
the kind of love that creates space
for peace and safety,
and happiness and joy

**your intuition is always there,
protecting you**

when you met him,
the inquisition began.

you questioned *it all.*

all that you already knew to be true.
about yourself, suddenly needed scrutiny.

so, i served as your constant reminder.
the voice of reason you'd soon abandon
to his unsubstantiated opinions and criticisms.

always steadfast and resolute.
repeating the same words. like a mantra.
attempting to break through
to you -

> *"love yourself first. remember who you are.
> and if he causes you to question that, run fast
> my love, run far"*

can you see now how we
set the galaxy on fire?

the universe of us folded
into a blaze. we burned it
to the ground. and now,
we wade through the soot
of what remains. praying
for the dust to settle

we should have known
this would happen.

our planets
collided with a spark. igniting
the whole of us. and the aftermath
and shock waves,
neither of us expected

and i wonder now -

how could we not know,
that together,
we were a roaring explosion?

why did we not
consider, that together,
we would go up in flames?

void

what remains

what remains, is not enough
to make me whole.
no matter how i try
to piece the remnants of us
together. again.

no peace can come from this

words fail the ways i've imagined you
in so many places,

my intimate spaces,
experiencing this life
next to me.

and i can only hope you understand my plea

instead, with every exasperated
confession from my lips, your steps quicken.
leading you further from me.
you find my revelation of feeling, revolting.
the declaration of my love,
repulsive to your ears.

and though i've tried,
i cannot stop
speaking my truth.
i cannot stop praying.
pleading. wishing.

hoping, my words
make room
for me, inside of you -
even as your sprint away creates distance
between us. placing you beyond my reach.

and i am now exhausted
with the evaporation of you

your shadow, scarcely visible
in this haze of relentless residue,

> *- the smoke that seeps from the sole of your shoes*
> *encapsulates everything –*

is fading. becoming elusive
to me.

there is nothing left
but your silhouette.
it's all i have now,

and it's all that remains.
of us.

the familiar nature of deceit

he sang a song
i found familiar.
whiskey heavy on his breath
and i knew he'd been
to a forbidden place
guilt rode high upon his chest

> she entered the room
> in silence.
> thighs fragrant with deceit
> eyes low.
> a slight smile
> and it all seemed strange to me

she hummed a tune
i found familiar
couldn't shake it
from my thoughts.
my mind raced time
to try and find
the memories
that melody brought

> he sang a song
> i found familiar.
> same one was sung to me
> when mama died
> and my soul cried
> and i struggled

just to breathe
i knew then,
where i heard the song.
remembered clear as day.
my sister
sang it when she held me close
and kissed the pain away

she sang it when she held me close
and kissed the pain away

empty promises lead to broken hearts

i blame you
for leading me here. out
in the middle of nowhere

how can this be home?
blank walls and no heat. cold.
sterile. making it easier for you to leave

you never intended to
share this space with me

> *this pit stop of sorts for you*

yet you question my questions
and argue indefensibly
that this was *my* choice
that i knew what you were.
and were not, to me

> *i didn't ask you to bring me here*

lured by your promise
of commitment and fidelity
painted walls. and a warm safe space
for you to love me

but instead,
you led me here. out
in the middle of nowhere

miseducated hearts

we learn unsolicited lessons in love,

> pop quizzes on:
>> *how to stay loyal*
>> *to the uncommitted*

> last minute essays on:
>> *the fantastical art of pretending*
>> *to be happy*

> and final exams on:
>> *fighting for someone*
>> *you'll never be enough for*

emerging broken. bruised. left for dead

the graduating class of wounded soldiers,
with honors in:
> *surviving the battlefield of love*

receiving an improper education
on matters of the heart
taught by those that never loved us

war

you brought anarchy
and discord

caused a complete rebellion
in my body

when my soul attempted to escape
to rid itself of you

heartbreakers are like the past

i realize now
you are like the past
no concern for how we could have ended,

had we done things differently

no regard
for what we may have become
what we should have been,

if only you had loved me

the sacrifice

you sacrificed a lifetime
for soft touches
and quiet whispers
secret moments
you say *made you feel important*

lost your soul
mate. your one
true love,

let forever slip away
for stolen kisses
and secret affections
that led you to an ecstasy
so brief, regret ran up your thigh
and lodged in your throat
with the last quiver of release

and you knew. before she knew
that there was no turning back
from this ledge. off which you'd leapt

let it fail

the breaking of us,
was a necessary action.
what we were,
was never worth saving.

we did irrevocable damage to each other.
it needed to burn
it needed to drown
it needed to fall apart

let it be
let it fail
let it go

metamorphosis of a heart breaker

heartache is a strange, savage thing.
the complete destruction of what was once safe.
secure. stable. *home.*

curated feelings. once heavy.
you now find easy to settle into.

so predictable. so dependable. in how it ends.
always. and in all ways
the same finale.

a consistent drain. you've learned to replenish
with what fills the body, never the heart.
refilling only on just-one-more-time sex.
empty again at the climax.

you're getting good at it now. managing
the aftermath of being slain. discovering yourself
in new ways, each time. the terrible
and the sweet.

there's a high
that shadows the breaking. euphoria
coated trauma, i call it.

careful not to overdose.
you're slowly becoming the ache
for someone else.

you are the haunting of me

yesterday, i tried a new café.
needed something different,
something out of the ordinary,
something new, *for me.*

drove out, further than normal.
thought i'd put some distance
between myself and our old ~~usual~~ spots.

found a vibrant café. an inviting place
in an area of town i recall you saying you didn't like.

imagine my heart. as i realized
everything on the menu,
you would have loved.
all your favorites listed
in bold. *taunting me.*

how quickly my smile waned
knowing, i was running into you
again. not in body,
but in thought.

these feelings always find me.
the constant thinking of you,
considering you… missing you.

the unending haunting of all of me,
by the harrowing memory of all of you.

heartache reveals what we don't want to

there are lessons in heartache.
lost love teaches.
reveals.
breaks
everything, without regard.
exposing the vulnerability in us
we wish didn't exist.

the undoneness of us

i often regret that we ended how we did
not with crying or screaming or fighting
or pleading or tearing each other apart

we ended in the most deafening silence

and now i can't help but wonder
what we left in the void
that formed between us

and now i can't stop thinking
about what went unsaid
all the words
we will never speak
to each other
all the words
that create
the undoneness of us

the breaking of you

the fact that it wasn't a grand gesture
doesn't mean it didn't break your heart.

it's not always the obvious offense
that sets the terror in motion.

in fact, i've learned,
sometimes it's the seemingly trivial actions
that compound. gathering
themselves together in the crevices.
the parts of you, you don't frequent often.
hiding, in plain sight.

so, you miss the surface scratches,
the ones that appear harmless. easy to manage.
the ones slowly forming a crack straight
down to the center of your heart.

it seems so palpable, now.
but for too long it went unnoticed,
and the damage has been done.

and now, it's strong. wreaking havoc
on all of you. finding it's way
to the deepest parts. cutting and splitting
and tearing things.

sometimes you feel it in the body.
a physical ache you can't describe.

sometimes your soul mourns
for the remnants, left behind.

pieces of the whole of you.

and you wonder how you missed it. the signs
of the coming rupture. the faint alarms
declaring the ruin that was to come.

how did you miss it?
how did you not see you were soiling
what was once beautiful? ...breeding
the very violence that would
come to consume you?

why did it take the breaking of you?
the vicious escape
of what you held most dear,
for you to finally see
the value in me?

comprehending the deceit of you

i pause my thoughts
press rewind
replaying each memory
a thousand times

stuck in wonder
trying to find
the exact moment
i failed to notice the signs

how could you keep the secret?
...that this was all just a lie?

why didn't you tell me
your heart was never mine?

please teach me too, before you go

saying goodbye was sticky on my tongue.
an unnatural act. a permanent declaration.
which left me

with immediate and unspeakable regret.

saying goodbye didn't unlearn your name
from my memories. didn't erase your scent
from my dreams.

and people never really go away completely. do they?

because. how could you really be gone,
and my heart not understand?

because. how could you leave me,
and not teach me to unlove us too?

the shallow truth of the words you speak

we survive, here.
where words are empty,
and hold no value.

a barren land, where
i need you –
never means
i'll do whatever it takes to keep you near.

a dark place, where
i love you –
doesn't translate to
i am yours, forever.

a void, where
i miss you –
won't ever be
i'm coming, and this time i promise to never leave.

celestial

to all the lovers who lost me

my hands long to write
to you. all the lovers
who lost - me.

a sharp reminder
of what you threw away. abused.
discarded without hesitation.

my fingers tip toe
about the keyboard. finding letters.
creating the words i ~~want~~ need
to say.

for the times i was called out of my name.
told i was not enough. struck
by hard knuckles and open palms.
asked to leave. and forced by your force
to believe your lies.

i don't dare give these syllables escape
from my lips.
spoken words manifest reality.

instead, i write.
of the many times
i thought my heart was broken,
convinced myself
i was wounded, tragically.

another lie, i unfortunately believed.

when pieces create a masterpiece

grateful now
to have emerged
in pieces
so that i can discover
my whole self
despite, you

next time, we'll always meet at your place

i convince myself in fact and fiction
there is nothing more of you left.
that i am whole. complete. ready, without you.

theories i can't quantify

there are reminders everywhere
couldn't sell off everything, i tried.

and why did we create so many memories here
anyway?

should've wondered why you always came
to me. should've read between the lines.

because now, i experience your invasion. daily.

a constant encounter of you,
causes my new self
        - my healed and i don't need you self -
to fail again and again.

even though you are not present, in body.
you. are. everywhere.

i'm a new woman now. everyone can see it.
took classes that made me better.
but could not make me better

placed an altar where your favorite chair
used to sit, all obnoxious and proud.
took back ownership of my space.
had to remind myself
that it once was *my own space.*

and still, your residue endures

i feel you sometimes. see your eyes
in the shadows. never ending reminders
that you're still here. lingering.
lurking. haunting me.

and every day i thoroughly convince myself,
there is nothing more of you left.
that i am whole. complete. ready, without you.

that time i didn't recognize my own heart

my heart has been ravaged
so many times,
by you

i barely recognized it, myself

until i found a trace
of the brand
you seared into it

and knew that it was mine

my heart cannot be convinced

i've explained to my heart
that it's time to move on.
asked my mind to omit all of you

can't change a decision i didn't make
        -   i remind my thoughts

and it is this reality that lacerates me.
years, lost. to what once was us

a constant ambush of memory and emotion.
and the exhausting convincing of self
that you won't ever return

sometimes letting someone go, sets you free

i used to question myself.
kept wondering what was wrong
with me. always considering
how to be better. how to be more.
how to be perfect,
for you

thought if i could prove my love.
prove myself
worthy,
of you.
that you would never leave

now when, i think back
on those moments -
the broken, sad desperation
of my former self -
i ask my memories why
i ever wanted you to stay

unquestionable

letting go of wrong
will always be right

you leaving, was an introduction to me

when you left,
i was scared. anxious.
filled with fear
at the thought of being alone.
of being lonely.
of being abandoned,
by you

and when you were gone
i was finally free. open
to the possibility
of learning
and discovering,
for myself,
how to be loved
by me

life always resembles life

to heal you need a garden

         – she spoke softly,
           in nearly a whisper.

fill it with seeds of plants and spicy herbs
and flowering bushes. and each day
as they grow and flourish
you will too

when the flowers begin to blossom
and the fruit dangles from its stem
that is the moment
you will also begin to bloom

first, i need a moment to heal

i realize now
it may be too late for me

i'm slightly bruised and a bit torn

my heart's been broken
so many times. i'm afraid
my ability to give love is now distorted

and i'm no longer sure
about much of anything.
especially not who to love next.
especially not how to love myself

the tangible shadow of memories

i'm surprised
at how vividly i dreamt you
how all your details came to life

how the thought of you
warmed my skin
and quickened my heart

complete sensory invasion

until my mind recalled
your absence and the grief
of your departure

and i wonder
when the ache in my soul,
will liberate me too

i was the loneliest when i was with you

for too long, i feared
the thought
of being alone

so, i stayed.
creating the loneliest reality
of all

> *by not cutting ties to the thing*
> *that held me down.*

> *by not giving myself permission*
> *to let you go.*

the difficulty of healing

this healing, after
you, has been rough.
on my face
on my mind
on my heart

coming back to yourself is a process

why is this so painful?

> – she cried. voice breaking.
> pressured by emotion

like a festering wound. sometimes the healing of
your flesh hurts more than the injury itself

> – i told her. wisdom heavy on my tongue

the coming back together of you is a process.
raw at first, exposed and sensitive. so, you cleanse it,
wrap it gently, and protect it from further harm.

you apply a salve to ease the pain.

but it's the tightening that tests your tolerance.
the way skin unhurriedly heals. itchy and tender.
needing to breathe.

so, you uncover it. exposed. unveiled. vulnerable.

and you are fierce in the guarding of this wounded part
of you. until the scab flakes away
no longer needing protecting. until you've healed
enough... touch no longer sets the wound ablaze.

manifesting love doesn't always happen how you imagined

not all hurtful experiences are the end.
and things are not always as they seem.

sometimes, the breaking of you is necessary.
an unavoidable process, challenging you
to manifest a finer version of self. a variant of sorts.

creating a you that is ready and deserving
and capable of accepting
the physical manifestation
of your heart's deepest desire.

the one whose human design fits perfectly
with yours. a divine connection. a love aligned.

the one who once inhabited your dreams
and made a home in the hope of, 'what if'

what if, you require a breaking to be...
free of what is no longer necessary?

what if enduring loss, is preparation
for what is truly meant to be?

letting go set me free

i thought i lost myself
when you left.
doubtlessly believed
i was irrevocably broken.

but as my heart grew strong,
and my thoughts became clear,
and feelings faded
i came to understand, the truth.

letting go of us
didn't break me at all

actually, letting go
of us was the catalyst
that set me free.

above all, i wish you well

i've always wanted nothing less
than the best for you. i realize now
how i pushed you to be the best
version of yourself. a version of you,
you couldn't envision. a version of you,
you could never embody.

you taught me
potential is often
only seen outside of yourself.
and i know this
because you never
did see, or accept,
the full possibility
of who you could be

and i hope with all my heart
you find someone that understands,
your insecurities.

someone that won't require you
to be more. than who you'll allow
yourself to be.

someone who will accept you,
diminished and inadequate,
knowing who you are now
is the very best you will ever be.

the memory of us is enough

i never want to forget you
or the love we had together,
i only seek to heal enough,
to one day love the memory
of you. to one day smile
at the memory
of us.

this isn't the life i dreamed of

everyday i miss you more
than the one before
but today, has been especially difficult
because no matter what i do,
it's a constant reminder
that i'm living a life meant for two,
without you

perihelion

i can't be the housewife you need me to be

honestly, i regret it. all
these dreadful decisions, made in haste.
no need to persist, now.

prefer to face the consequences. be made
an example of, then embody
this shell, now insignificant.

break me open for all to see. strip me
bare. slice me deep. carve me
to the bone.

i want to watch you loose
the vestigial souls.
that made this body a home.

set me ablaze. let me smolder
to ash. then, float me
out to the sea.

free from this dreaded place.
and this curse,
you cast on me.

because, i'll never be
the housewife
you need me to be.

getting familiar with being alone

here i lay. holding this cold jelly thing
to my temple. it loses its cool too fast.
doesn't last long enough to help
with the pain. the throbbing,

isn't getting any better.
three Goody powders later,
lights off. devices muted. and still
here i lay
thinking of sage advice
given by my mother's mother -

something about being good to yourself
even when no one else is around. something about
caring for yourself like you would care for a lover.
or, like a good man would care for you.

and i wonder in silence, what he'd say
to me in this moment. my non-existent lover.
my *good man*. i try to picture him
loving me through this throb
in my head, his whispers in my ear -

"are you okay my love?
can i rub your neck?
let me hold you
until the pain goes away"

when you let a good thing get away

he says he thinks of me all the time
especially during the holidays.
and he's annoyed. because it's been a while
now. and his parents still ask about me.
says he thought he'd be better by now.
healed and moved on.

he's so confused.

i think nobody told him
how difficult it can be
to mend a broken heart
when it's actually broken.

i don't think
he was ever really in love,
before

says maybe he should come over.
we should talk. *again.*
try to understand what went wrong
says he just needs to see me. in person

and in this moment,
although he is the one
who left, he is also the one
with the most regret

a star among stars

you are not an unturned stone
waiting to be discovered.
found. refined.

you are a star among stars
an illuminating energy

perfectly positioned
for the right eye
to finally see.

the life of a woman

where i come from being a woman is hard
work. a constant labor. always something
to be done. for someone
other than yourself -

has he been fed?
have they been cleaned?
is my house in order?
was there enough sex this week?

one day

one day. love will come
for you. not as the fairy-tale
you've imagined.

you are not a damsel in distress
waiting to be saved

one day. love will come
for you. and it be everything
you desire.

not a perfect love.
perfection is a myth.
but a love that gives,
restores, and replenishes.

the perfect love, for you

you could never be too much
you're still being created

there is never enough
of you. how could you be too much, my love?
when the creation of you is not yet finished.

a constant work-in-progress. a delicate
project. being made and unmade. done
and undone. broken and pieced together.

infinite possibilities
building you, improving you,
making you more
than what you were before.

again and again
without end

i was here first

one day, you will understand
why i am my own first love.
because before there was
a you and i
and nothing was right
with this world,
the only person that loved me
and never let me down
the only person that loved me
and didn't walk away
was me

you are the special thing

it's okay to guard your energy
to protect your heart and your mind

>>> not everyone is deserving of your presence
>>> or the revelations hidden in your truths

it's perfectly fine to not to share your magic.
your secrets. your time

>>> to be selfish and intentional and deliberate
>>> in the act of protecting what is special about you

ethereal

let's be nothing and everything

let's be.
nothing
to the universe
but everything to each other.
so intertwined,
there is no defining line
between you and i

let's be.
a hurricane
massive and fierce.
we'll usher in the storm surge
and meet in the eye
where all is calm
and all is beautiful

let's be.
the sunset
alchemy in motion.
luring light from the sky
embracing the twilight
kissing the end of the world.
with eternity on our side

let's be

love is an action verb

true love isn't a fairy-tale
summed up in happy endings
or a single kiss that makes all that's wrong,
suddenly right.

true love is action. a verb.
it shows up. in the little things.
in private moments
in not-so-pretty memories.

true love is someone holding parts of you
together - when you're unable or unwilling –
without fail. or conditions.
or resentment.

true love is the determination of a lover
to help you find peace
among the pieces. refusing,
to let you fall apart.

the aging of love

how could i become bored
with you, when the universe awaits us?
a world of possibilities
tugging at our hearts
infinite happiness
calling us home

there's so much more for me to be, with you

new things to see,
to experience,
to feel

a new me to be,
to *become*
with you

when you've found your person

i caught myself staring
at your picture, today.
even though you were near

just a room away

and i realized then,
your smile captured on paper
is enough,
to make everything better
with me

let's keep it simple today

today, let's rest
                    in each other
limbs on limbs
                    skin to skin

                                        no beginning to you
                                        and to me no end

today, let's relax
            without distraction
soft linen heavy with our scent
                    tongues sweet
with the taste of us

                                        quiet storms
                            and peach mimosas on repeat

today, let's enjoy
            the melody of us
fall in love with the harmony
            our voices create together
mouths full. overflowing with,
            i love you
            and i love you too

always in his corner

he *felt* heavy. weighted.
run down, by the hand he's been dealt

the world is wearing him
thin. but he is strong.
and he is brave.

i heard his voice crack, as he described his day.
and my soul ached watching him
straighten his face
quickly. erasing any sign of pain.

he worries in secret. camouflages stress
with laughter. thinks he disguises it well.

but i still see.
i always know.

so i hold him close in the night and remind him
of exactly who he is. tell him everything
will be okay.

then, i tell him what is true -

> *you are magnificently made, perfectly designed.*
> *if anyone was created for greatness, my love, it is you*

i love the whole of you, even if you don't

i've come to terms
with a particular fact
you just don't see yourself,
the way i see you

your face still folds
into uneasy distortion
when i compliment the things i love most
about you

and somehow you don't understand
aren't quite able to comprehend
how all the things you don't see
- or have chosen not to believe -

the parts of yourself
you've become blind to

are all the things
i desire most
are all the things
i cannot be without

there is peace in the eye of the storm of you

love is
running into the storm
of someone else's chaos
and finding peace
right in the center
because for you
it all makes sense

the serenity of him

he overwhelmed my chaos
with an indescribable calm
and instantly i knew,
without doubt or fear,
that i had found my home

it's the wind that scares me the most

there aren't many things
that give me pause
but i am deathly afraid of the wind
and the possibility of being carried away,
from you.

of the thought of never seeing you again

she is enough

she is a star
within a galaxy
and still,
she is all he sees
when he gazes
out into the vastness
of the universe

they will know

the one,
who is deserving,
of you
will see you.

will complement your wholeness.

will be drawn
to only you,
to your magic,
to your heart.
and will find you
despite everything.

despite the noise
and the distractions.

despite the crowded,
infinite landscape
of the universe.

planet of me
universe of us

we exist in a universe. *together,*
solitary planets. in incessant orbit
of one another.

glancing out
around moons and stars,
seeking a momentary glimpse.
squinting through sun fire.

for assurance
the other is still there

i want to play
in your oceans and plant seeds
on your lands. smile in rainbows
and imagine your trees are your hands

but you are there and i am here -

always close enough to see
never so near to touch

and i think i'm okay now
with risking everything.
imploding into a ball of fire.
if it means i could find my way
to you

for you my love...

you, are where i belong.
when apart from us,
i find myself lost.
completely displaced.
because with you,
i am safe and loved.
because in you,
i have made my home.

thank you

You are here. You've completed this poetic journey with me and I am so very grateful to have shared this collection with you.

If you've enjoyed this book, please leave a 5-star review on the site where your purchased your copy or on sincerelytiffanynicole.com. I read every review and repost every photo submitted. But even more importantly, each review helps new readers discover my books.

Let's continue the journey. Don't miss reader exclusives, sneak peaks, special announcements, or book updates. Sign up to keep in touch at: sincerelytiffanynicole.com

Follow me: Instagram: @sincerelytiffanynicole

sincerely Tiffany Nicole

ALSO AVAILABLE NOW

ON MY
BEST DAY

On My Best Day is the ultimate self-love anthem, from the personal writings of lifelong poet Tiffany Nicole Pigée, for the healing of your mind, your soul, your spirit, and your heart.

...exhausted. with this day that never ends. running in and out of myself. looking for me in you. even my soul knows it's not where it's supposed to be —

Planet of Me
of Me
Universe
of Us